Read-About® Geography

# Arkansas

## By Nancy Leber

**Consultant**
Nanci R. Vargus, Ed.D.
Assistant Professor of Literacy
University of Indianapolis, Indianapolis, Indiana

Children's Press®
A Division of Scholastic Inc.
New York   Toronto   London   Auckland   Sydney
Mexico City   New Delhi   Hong Kong
Danbury, Connecticut

Designer: Herman Adler Design
Photo Researcher: Caroline Anderson
The photo on the cover shows Sugarloaf Mountain and the Little Red River.

**Library of Congress Cataloging-in-Publication Data**

Leber, Nancy.
  Arkansas / by Nancy Leber.
    p. cm. – (Rookie read-about geography)
Includes index.
Summary: Introduces the state of Arkansas and its diverse geographical
features, wildlife, and more.
  ISBN 0-516-22746-7 (lib. bdg.)    0-516-27946-7 (pbk.)
  1. Arkansas–Juvenile literature. 2. Arkansas–Geography–Juvenile literature.
[1. Arkansas.] I. Title. II. Series.
  F411.3.L43 2004
  917.6'7–dc22

                                                    2003016898

# Which state has a diamond mine you can visit?

Arkansas has one!

Arkansas is in the south central United States.

Can you find it on this map?

CANADA

WASHINGTON
OREGON
IDAHO
MONTANA
NORTH DAKOTA
SOUTH DAKOTA
MINNESOTA
WISCONSIN
MICHIGAN
NEW HAMPSHIRE
VERMONT
MAINE
NEW YORK
MASSACHUSETTS
RHODE ISLAND
CONNECTICUT
NEW JERSEY
DELAWARE
MARYLAND
Washington, D.C.
PENNSYLVANIA
OHIO
WEST VIRGINIA
VIRGINIA
NEVADA
UTAH
COLORADO
KANSAS
NEBRASKA
IOWA
ILLINOIS
INDIANA
MISSOURI
KENTUCKY
TENNESSEE
NORTH CAROLINA
SOUTH CAROLINA
CALIFORNIA
ARIZONA
NEW MEXICO
OKLAHOMA
ARKANSAS
ALABAMA
GEORGIA
WYOMING
TEXAS
MISSISSIPPI
LOUISIANA
FLORIDA

North
West    East
South

ALASKA    CANADA

MEXICO

HAWAII

5

Cavern in the Ozark Mountains

Arkansas has mountains, lakes, and forests. It is a great place to fish, canoe, or hike.

The Ozark Mountains are in Arkansas. People like to explore the caves there.

The Ozarks have cold springs. Springs are streams of water that come up from the ground. Spring water is good to drink.

The Ouachita (WAH-shuh-taw) Mountains are in the northwest. The highest point in Arkansas is Mount Magazine.

Bobcat

Deer, black bears, wolves, and bobcats live in these mountains.

Hot Springs National Park is in the Ouachita Mountains.

Some people take baths in the hot spring water or sniff the steam.

13

The Oauchitas also have diamonds.

Finder's keepers! If you dig for diamonds and find one, it's yours!

The land in eastern
Arkansas is low and flat.
This makes it good for
farming.

Farmers in Arkansas grow
rice and cotton. They raise
chickens, too.

# Many people in Arkansas work in the food business.

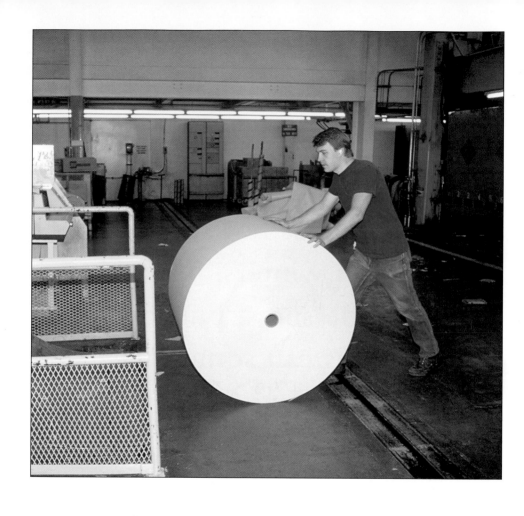

Others make things such
as paper.

Arkansas has hot summers and mild winters. There is very little snow, but lots of rain. This can sometimes cause flooding.

22

Thick pine forests cover southern Arkansas. Pine is the state tree. Wood and paper are made from these trees.

Many kinds of birds live there. The American bald eagle is one of them.

Southern Arkansas also has lakes and bayous. Bayous are swampy parts of rivers. Alligators and many birds live there.

The state bird is the
mockingbird.

Little Rock is the largest city in Arkansas. It is also the state capital. The Arkansas River flows through Little Rock.

Little Rock

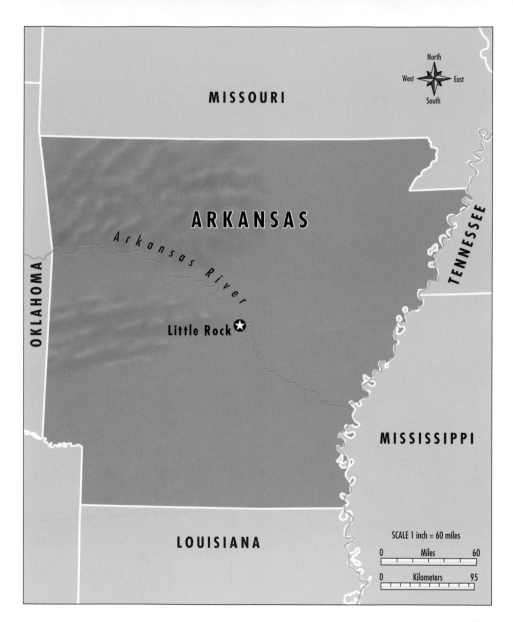

MISSOURI

North
West ✦ East
South

ARKANSAS

OKLAHOMA

*Arkansas River*

Little Rock ⭐

TENNESSEE

MISSISSIPPI

LOUISIANA

SCALE 1 inch = 60 miles

0          Miles          60

0        Kilometers        95

27

Many people come to
Arkansas to hear the
music and see the crafts.
They like the bubbly
springs and the state fair.

What do you like most
about Arkansas?

29

# Words You Know

bobcat

cave

diamond mine

hot springs

in ouachita
mountain

Little Rock

mockingbird

Mount Magazine

pine trees

31

# Index

# About the Author

Nancy Leber is an editor and writer. She lives in New York City.

# Photo Credits

Photographs © 2004: AP/Wide World: 21 (J.Ross Jones), 15, 28, 30 bottom left (Danny Johnston); Arkansas Department of Parks & Tourism/Chuck Haralson: 6, 16, 30 top right; Dembinsky Photo Assoc.: 11, 30 top left (Claudia Adams), 25, 31 top right (Gary Meszaros); Photo Researchers, NY: cover (Dennis Flaherty), 12, 22, 30 bottom right, 31 bottom right (Garry D. McMichael); PhotoEdit: 19 (Tony Freeman), 18 (Don Smetzer); Stock Boston: 26, 31 top left (John Elk III); Visuals Unlimited: 3 (Mark Gibson), 9, 10, 31 bottom left (H.W. Robison).

Maps by Bob Italiano